Animal Athletes

Izzi Howell

Crabtree Publishing Company
www.crabtreebooks.com

CRABTREE
PUBLISHING COMPANY
WWW.CRABTREEBOOKS.COM

Author:
Izzi Howell
Editorial director:
Kathy Middleton
Editor:
Izzi Howell
Proofreaders:
Sonya Newland, Crystal Sikkens
Graphic design:
Clare Nicholas
Image research:
Izzi Howell
Production coordinator and prepress:
Tammy McGarr
Print coordinator:
Katherine Berti

Images:
Alamy: Jerome Murray - CC 6, Anthony Pierce 19c, blickwinkel 23b, Nature Picture Library 26, Minden Pictures 27t; Getty: Ian Dyball title page t and 28, OceanBodhi 12t, Ian_Redding 12b, semet 13, Michael Zeigler 15t, GlobalP 15c, Anna segeren 19t, coopder1 20, wasantistock 25, HeitiPaves 27b, stylep_de 3 and 29t; Nature Picture Library: Bertie Gregory/2020VISION 7b, Franco Banfi 14, Andy Rouse 17b, Tony Wu 18–19b, Stephen Dalton 21l, Premaphotos 22, Solvin Zankl 27bl; Shutterstock: Eric Isselee title page c and 24, Lukas Walter title page b and 10, Dr Ajay Kumar Singh 4, Leon Marais 5, Collins93 7t, Elana Erasmus 8, JonathanC Photography 9tl and 31, nwdph 9tr, Alessandro De Maddalena 11t, Fiona Ayerst 11b, RomanYa 15b, sitayi 16, Volodymyr Burdiak 17t, Songquan Deng 21r, Jiri Prochazka 23t, Andre Marais 29b.

Library and Archives Canada Cataloguing in Publication

Title: Animal athletes / Izzi Howell.
Names: Howell, Izzi, author.
Description: Series statement: Astonishing animals |
  Includes bibliographical references and index.
Identifiers: Canadiana (print) 20200155067 | Canadiana (ebook) 20200155075 |
  ISBN 9780778769156 (hardcover) |
  ISBN 9780778769330 (softcover) |
  ISBN 9781427124333 (HTML)
Subjects: LCSH: Animal locomotion—Juvenile literature. |
  LCSH: Animal mechanics—Juvenile literature.
Classification: LCC QP301 .H69 2020 | DDC j591.5/7—dc23

Library of Congress Cataloging-in-Publication Data

Names: Howell, Izzi, author.
Title: Animal athletes / Izzi Howell.
Description: New York : Crabtree Publishing Company, [2020] |
  Series: Astonishing animals | Includes index.
Identifiers: LCCN 2019053185 (print) | LCCN 2019053186 (ebook) |
  ISBN 9780778769156 (hardcover) |
  ISBN 9780778769330 (paperback) |
  ISBN 9781427124333 (ebook)
Subjects: LCSH: Animal locomotion--Juvenile literature. | Animals--Miscellanea--
  Juvenile literature. | Animal mechanics--Juvenile literature.
Classification: LCC QP301 .H767 2020 (print) | LCC QP301 (ebook) |
  DDC 591.5/7--dc23
LC record available at https://lccn.loc.gov/2019053185
LC ebook record available at https://lccn.loc.gov/2019053186

Crabtree Publishing Company

www.crabtreebooks.com   1-800-387-7650

Printed in the U.S.A./022020/CG20200102

Published in Canada
Crabtree Publishing
616 Welland Ave.
St. Catharines, Ontario
L2M 5V6

Published in the United States
Crabtree Publishing
PMB 59051
350 Fifth Avenue, 59th Floor
New York, New York 10118

Published in the United Kingdom
Crabtree Publishing
Maritime House
Basin Road North, Hove
BN41 1WR

Published in Australia
Crabtree Publishing
Unit 3 – 5 Currumbin Court
Capalaba
QLD 4157

Table of contents

Animal athletes 4

Peregrine falcons 6

Cheetahs 8

Shortfin mako sharks 10

Octopuses 12

California sea lions 14

Impalas 16

Spinner dolphins 18

Fleas 20

Horned dung beetles 22

Ants 24

Cuvier's beaked whales 26

Rüppell's griffon vultures 28

Glossary 30

Find out more 31

Index 32

Animal athletes

Athletes display extreme speed, mind-boggling flexibility, and super strength...animal athletes, that is! Athletic abilities are a huge advantage in the animal kingdom, helping them catch **prey** and avoid becoming prey themselves! In many cases, animals take the gold medal and outperform human athletes.

Astonishing abilities

Jaw-dropping animal athletes include the speedy sprinters, such as cheetahs, which can run, fly, or swim at incredible speeds. Then there are the acrobats, such as octopuses, with incredibly flexible bodies that twist into amazing shapes. Champion jumpers, such as fleas, reach huge heights—sometimes many times taller than they are!

Both the cheetah and the wildebeest are among the fastest land animals, but the cheetah is just a little bit quicker! Only the fastest and luckiest wildebeest can escape from cheetahs.

Phenomenal feats

The weightlifters of the animal kingdom, such as ants, are able to carry huge loads—even on remarkably small bodies. Other animals are able to soar in the sky as high as a plane, or dive huge depths beneath the waves.

An elephant can lift objects up to 660 pounds (300 kg) in weight with just its trunk. That's as heavy as 45 bowling balls!

Peregrine falcons

What is the fastest animal on Earth? Did you say cheetah? Close, but not quite! The fastest animal in the world is actually the peregrine falcon. This **bird of prey** can dive at speeds of over 200 miles per hour (322 kph)—as fast as the top speed of some race cars!

Spot and stoop

Peregrine falcons have incredible eyesight. They soar high in the sky, scanning for prey flying below them. Once they have spotted their prey, they rush down to attack. This move is known as a "stoop." The peregrine falcon catches its prey in mid-air and uses its **talons** to break its prey's neck.

The peregrine falcon changes its shape as it dives so that it can move faster through the air.

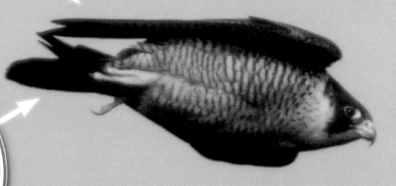

The falcon tucks in its tail and feet, and pulls back its wings so that its body has a smooth, **streamlined** shape.

Wow!

A peregrine falcon's eyesight is eight times better than a human's, allowing the bird to spot prey from nearly 2 miles (3 km) away!

FACT FILE

Found in:
Every continent except Antarctica

Habitat:
Cliffs, grasslands, cities, and many other places

Length: 14–20 inches (35–50 cm) with a wingspan of around 3.2 feet (1 m)

Diet: Small and medium-sized birds

New homes

Many of the places where peregrine falcons used to live, such as forests, have been cut down to build houses. So peregrine falcons have found unlikely new homes in cities! They like to nest on high buildings, such as skyscrapers, power stations, and cathedrals.

This peregrine falcon's nest is high above the streets of London, UK. This spot is a great place to watch for prey, such as pigeons, and even crows.

Cheetahs

Which animal can accelerate as fast as a sports car? From 0 to 70 miles per hour (113 kph) in just three seconds, the cheetah is the fastest land animal!

The cheetah has a large heart that pumps a lot of blood to its muscles. This gives more energy to its body so that it can run quickly.

Top speed sprinting

The cheetah uses its excellent vision to search for prey. It waits for its prey to get close and then it pounces, bursting into a speedy sprint! Its top speed chase is usually over quickly. Moving so fast, cheetahs only have the energy to cover about 650 to 1,000 feet (198 to 304 m).

The cheetah's long legs help it to reach high speeds.

Keeping its balance

If a cheetah's prey darts from side to side, the cheetah is able to make quick turns to follow it. Its long tail helps it to balance as it swerves around corners!

Cheetahs dig their long claws into the ground to stop themselves from slipping.

Wow!

The cheetah is so fast that its chase is usually over in less than one minute.

Shortfin mako sharks

If you thought razor-sharp teeth and a deadly bite were scary, how about adding super speed to the list? The shortfin mako shark is the fastest shark in the world, reaching speeds of 43 miles per hour (69 kph).

Super swift swimmers

The shark's pointed snout helps it to cut through the water, so it uses less energy to push itself forward.

Pursuing prey

The shortfin mako shark's prey, such as tuna and swordfish, are some of the fastest fish in the ocean. These sharks need to be even faster if they're going to catch a meal! Once a shortfin mako shark has caught a fish, it bites its tail off so that it can't escape. This helps the shark save energy for speedy swimming later on.

The smooth texture of the shortfin mako shark's skin reduces **friction** from the water. This, along with its streamlined body, helps it move quickly through the water.

At risk

Sadly, the shortfin mako shark is **endangered**. Its population has decreased because people are hunting too many sharks for their meat and fins. **Conservationists** hope that governments will pass laws to protect them.

Wow!

Engineers have used sharkskin, such as that of the shortfin mako shark, as inspiration for bathing-suit fabric to help competitive swimmers race faster!

FACT FILE

Found in: Tropical and cool oceans

Length: 10–12 feet (3–3.7 m)

Diet: Fish, squid, and other sharks

A fisherman releases a young mako shark that has been accidentally caught. Putting young sharks back into the water helps the population to recover, as these young sharks can later **reproduce**.

Octopuses

How small a hole could an animal squeeze through if it didn't have any bones? Look at an octopus for the answer! With no bones to get in the way, an octopus can pack itself into the tiniest of spaces!

Most octopuses use their beaks to feed on shellfish, prawns, and fish.

Octopuses swim, crawl, or push themselves forward by shooting out jets of water behind them.

This is part of the hard structure inside an octopus's beak.

Soft and squishy

The octopus has an almost entirely soft body! It is made from soft **tissue** that can stretch, lengthen, and change shape. The only hard part of its body is the beak around its mouth. It uses its beak to attack and kill its prey.

Octopuses can camouflage, or change color, to match their surroundings. They use camouflage to hide from **predators** such as fish, whales, and sea birds.

Hide and seek

The size of an octopus's beak is its only limit to squeezing through holes, as its beak has to fit through, too! Octopuses hide in small spaces where predators can't follow them, such as cracks in rocks or inside empty shells. They even hang out inside human garbage in the oceans, such as glass bottles.

An octopus can fit inside almost any object, as long as there is enough space inside for its curled-up body!

Wow!

A 595-pound (270-kg) octopus can squeeze through an opening with a diameter of 1 inch (2.5 cm).

1-inch
← (2.5 cm) →
diameter

California sea lions

Imagine an animal that can bend so far backward that its head reaches its feet! This is just one of the many acrobatic abilities of the California sea lion. Its flexibility helps it catch prey in all directions underwater.

Flexible fish hunters

Even when bent, the body of the California sea lion is still smooth and streamlined. This means it doesn't slow down as it changes direction underwater.

California sea lions use their long front flippers to push themselves forward. Their back flippers help them steer from side to side.

You can't catch me!

California sea lions aren't the fastest swimmers, but their flexibility allows them to make quick turns. They bend their body and neck to change direction. This helps them easily follow their prey, which often makes sudden turns to try to escape. Better luck next time!

It is hard for California sea lions to walk smoothly on their flippers, which makes them less graceful on land than they are in water.

Sea to land

California sea lions come out of the water in groups called **colonies** to **breed** and give birth. Their flexibility helps them move around on land, too. Out of the water, their back flippers rotate to face forward so they can walk on all four legs!

Wow!

California sea lions can dive to depths of 1,000 feet (305 m) if they can't find food higher up. That's as deep as the Eiffel Tower is tall!

Impalas

Would you feel a little jumpy if you knew a lion was lurking nearby? Impalas use their jumpiness as an advantage. Their sky-high jumps help them escape from predators on the African savannah.

A jumpy escape

Impalas are at risk from predators, such as lions and cheetahs, because they live in open areas with few hiding places. Living in large groups gives them some protection, but their incredible athletic jumping ability is key to their survival! If they are chased, the herd runs and jumps in many different directions. This confuses the predator, which doesn't know which impala to chase.

When an impala notices a predator, it barks an alarm to warn the rest of the herd.

When running, impalas easily jump over anything in their path.

Super stotters

Impalas do a type of jump known as stotting. They lift all four legs off the ground at once, and bounce up and down. They often do this jump before they run away. Researchers think the impala might be showing predators that they are fit and healthy, and not worth chasing!

Wow!

Impalas can jump up to 9.8 feet (3 m) high and 32.8 feet (10 m) across! That's half as long as a bowling lane!

Spinner dolphins

If the animal kingdom awarded a gold medal for gymnastics, it would be easily won by the spinner dolphin. With complex leaps that can reach nearly 10 feet (3 m) and include multiple spins, this **mammal** is known for its acrobatic ability.

Jump and splash

Spinner dolphins jump out of the water regularly, spinning and twisting several times while in the air. They create huge splashes as they land back in the water. Creating a large splash helps a dolphin remove **parasites** from its body. It could also be a way of getting its muscles warmed up and ready for hunting.

This image captured a spinner dolphin's jump, from twists and turns to the final splash.

Pod talk

Spinner dolphins are **social** animals that live in groups called pods. Each pod contains several dozen to 1,000 dolphins. Researchers are studying the reasons for the dolphins' acrobatic jumps. They believe spinning and jumping could be a way for dolphins to communicate with each other. Some have found that each jump might have a different meaning, such as danger, interest in **mating**, expressing happiness, or just showing off!

Found in: Tropical oceans

Length: 5.9–6.8 feet (1.8–2.1 m)

Diet: Small fish, squid, and shrimp

Wow!

Spinner dolphins have been recorded spinning seven times in a single jump!

As soon as one spinner dolphin starts jumping, other dolphins in the pod often join in.

19

Fleas

Miniature movers

How do teeny, tiny fleas get on cats, dogs, birds, and other animals without using wings? The answer is simple: they jump!

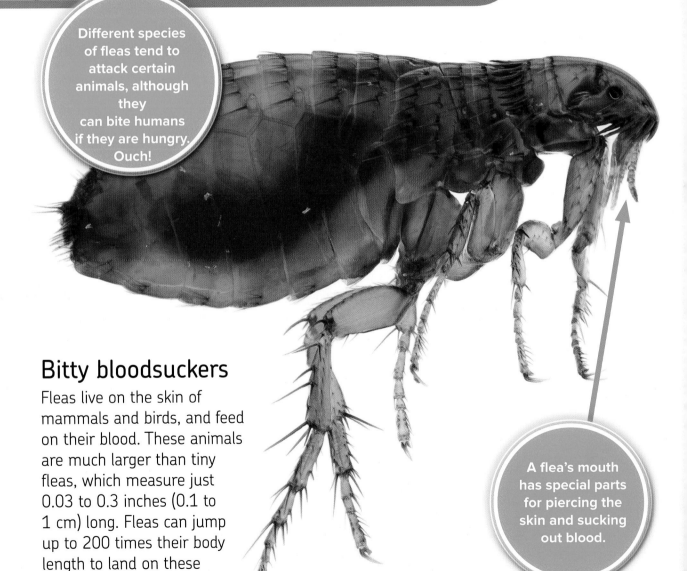

Different species of fleas tend to attack certain animals, although they can bite humans if they are hungry. Ouch!

A flea's mouth has special parts for piercing the skin and sucking out blood.

Bitty bloodsuckers

Fleas live on the skin of mammals and birds, and feed on their blood. These animals are much larger than tiny fleas, which measure just 0.03 to 0.3 inches (0.1 to 1 cm) long. Fleas can jump up to 200 times their body length to land on these big beasts.

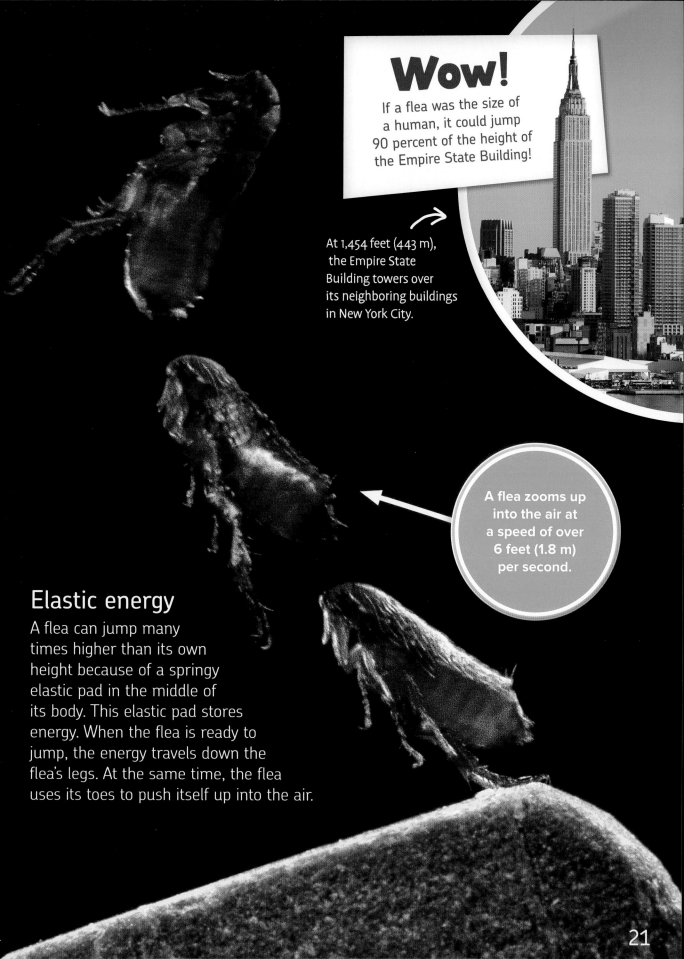

Wow!

If a flea was the size of a human, it could jump 90 percent of the height of the Empire State Building!

At 1,454 feet (443 m), the Empire State Building towers over its neighboring buildings in New York City.

A flea zooms up into the air at a speed of over 6 feet (1.8 m) per second.

Elastic energy

A flea can jump many times higher than its own height because of a springy elastic pad in the middle of its body. This elastic pad stores energy. When the flea is ready to jump, the energy travels down the flea's legs. At the same time, the flea uses its toes to push itself up into the air.

Horned dung beetles

Horned dung beetles roll **dung** into balls, while other species of dung beetle bury dung underground.

Could you pull the weight of six double-decker buses full of people? The male horned dung beetle could, if you made the buses beetle-sized! These tiny athletes can pull 1,141 times their own body weight. They use this strength to fight other beetles.

Dung tunnels

Horned dung beetles roll animal dung into round balls. The female beetles dig tunnels underneath the dung, in which their **young** will eventually live. While they are in the tunnels, young horned dung beetles live off nutrients from the dung—delicious! It's inside these tunnels that the male horned dung beetle's strength is put to the test!

Fighting for females

Male horned dung beetles need their super strength to defeat their rivals and mate with females. Mating takes place inside the tunnels dug by females. If a male enters a tunnel and another male is there, the two males wrestle with their horns, using their strength to try to push the other out of the tunnel. The strongest male wins the fight—and the female!

The strong horns of the horned dung beetle are tiny, measuring only a fraction of an inch.

Wow!

Some horned dung beetles do not have horns. They have to sneak in to mate before a beetle with horns catches them. Some even build secret side tunnels to get past the other males!

Ants

If you had to lift 10 to 50 times your own weight, which part of your body would you use? Your arms? Your back? How about your mouth? The super-strong jaws of ants allow them to carry incredible weights.

Jaw transportation

Ants use their jaws to carry objects that are much larger and heavier than they are. They bring useful objects, such as food, back to their nests. They also use their jaws for digging and cutting. Some species of ants have sticky feet, which help them to hang on when carrying heavy objects up walls.

Leafcutter ants carry pieces of leaf back to their nest. The leaves grow **fungus** inside the nest, which the ants eat.

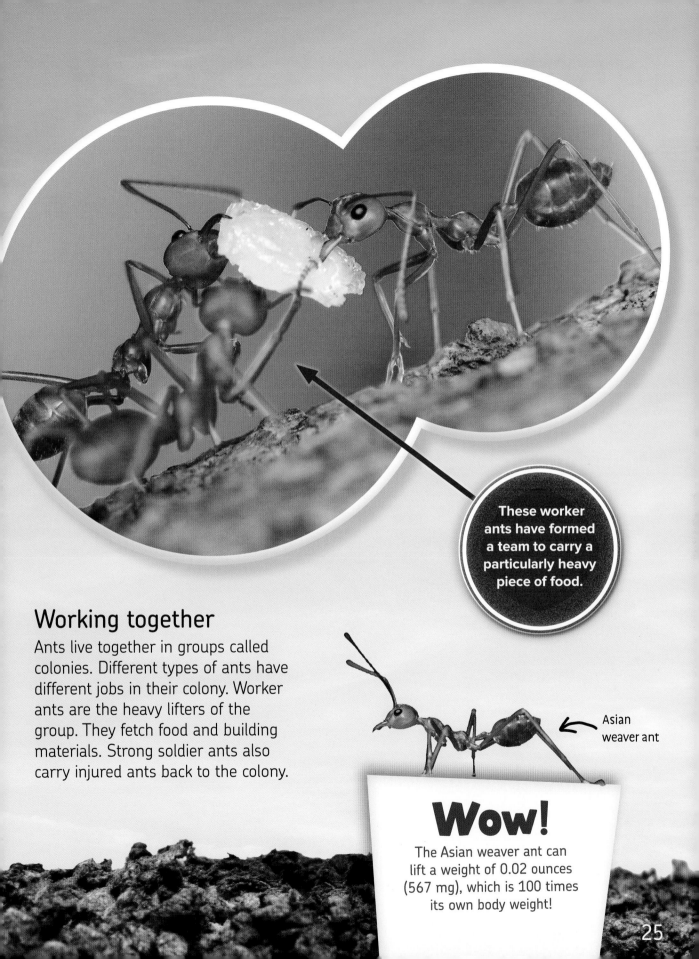

These worker ants have formed a team to carry a particularly heavy piece of food.

Working together

Ants live together in groups called colonies. Different types of ants have different jobs in their colony. Worker ants are the heavy lifters of the group. They fetch food and building materials. Strong soldier ants also carry injured ants back to the colony.

Asian weaver ant

Wow!

The Asian weaver ant can lift a weight of 0.02 ounces (567 mg), which is 100 times its own body weight!

Cuvier's beaked whales

Dazzling deep divers

Cuvier's beaked whales love to hunt and eat squid that live deep in the ocean. There's just one problem: it is nearly impossible for the whales to breathe so deep underwater, because all the water above pushes down on them. Luckily, Cuvier's beaked whales have incredible **adaptations** that allow them to dive deep and grab those scrumptious squid!

Under pressure

On their search for squid, Cuvier's beaked whales have reached depths of 9,816 feet (2,992 m). The **pressure** of the huge amounts of water above pushing down on them would be enough to pop their lungs, just like if you were to push hard on an inflated balloon. To stop this from happening, Cuvier's beaked whales breathe out almost all of the air in their lungs. This causes their lungs to lie flat—making them less likely to pop!

At just 3,280 feet (1,000 m) underwater, the pressure is 100 times greater than at the surface. Imagine what it must be like for Cuvier's beaked whale at three times that depth!

Surviving underwater

Whales are mammals, which means they need to breathe air. So how do Cuvier's beaked whales survive the long, deep dive with barely any **oxygen** in their lungs? The answer is by using only a very small amount of oxygen! Just a few important body parts, such as the heart, continue to receive oxygen to keep the whale alive.

FACT FILE

Found in: All deep oceans, except in polar areas

Length: 23 feet (7 m)

Diet: Squid and some fish

Cuvier's beaked whales store oxygen in their blood and muscles. They use this oxygen to give them a burst of energy when they need to chase tasty squid!

Wow!

A Cuvier's beaked whale can survive underwater for 138 minutes!

Cuvier's beaked whales eat deep-sea fish and squid, such as the cock-eyed squid.

Rüppell's griffon vultures

The blood of the Rüppell's griffon vulture is specially adapted to help them breathe at great heights, where there is little oxygen.

Rüppell's griffon vultures can spend six to seven hours in the sky each day, searching for food.

Did you know that most airplanes fly at around 36,000 feet (10,973 m) above sea level? What else would you expect to see at those heights? Some clouds? What about a Rüppell's griffon vulture? This is the highest-flying bird in the animal kingdom.

Searching and scavenging

Like other vultures, Rüppell's griffon vultures are **scavengers**. Rather than killing animals themselves, they eat animals that have already been killed by disease, old age, or other animals. By flying high in the skies, Rüppell's griffon vultures get the best view of dead animals on the ground below.

Wow!

Rüppell's griffon vultures are not affected by eating rotten meat infected with serious diseases such as cholera and anthrax! Strong acid in their stomachs destroys the bacteria that cause disease.

Tidying up

Rüppell's griffon vultures play an important role in the ecosystem. They quickly clean up dead animals by eating them, which helps to reduce the spread of disease.

Fights can break out when one vulture finds food. They hiss and grunt to scare away the other hungry vultures.

Rüppell's griffon vultures have no feathers on their head or neck to keep them from getting messy when digging in to their food.

These birds have very powerful beaks that can rip through skin and tear chunks of meat.

Glossary

adaptation Changes that make an animal more suited to its environment

bird of prey A large bird that kills smaller birds and animals for food

breed To reproduce and have young (for an animal)

colony A group of the same type of animals that live together

conservationist Someone who works to protect animals and the environment from human activity

dung Solid waste from a large animal

endangered Describes an animal or plant that is at risk of becoming extinct, because there are few of them still alive. When a species is extinct, it means its last surviving animal has died.

flexibility The ability to bend easily

friction When two surfaces rub against each other, making movement more difficult

fungus A group of living things that include mushrooms and mold

mammal A type of animal of which the females usually give birth to live young and feed them milk from their own body

mating Reproducing in order to have young

oxygen A gas in the air that animals and humans need to survive

parasite An animal that lives on another animal and feeds from it

predator An animal that hunts another animal for food

pressure The force of the weight of a liquid pushing against something

prey An animal that is hunted and killed for food by other animals

reproduce To have young

scavenger An animal that eats dead animals that have died naturally or been killed by other animals

social Describes an animal that lives together with other animals of the same species in an organized way

streamlined Describes something with a smooth, pointed shape that can move easily through water or air

talon A sharp claw on a bird's foot

tissue A material that living things' bodies are made from

young An animal's babies

Find out more

Books

Mattern, Joanne. *Animal Athletes*. Red Chair Press, 2019.

Thomas, Isobel. *Animalympics* series. Raintree, 2016.

Wassner, Sarah and Furgang, Kathy. *Animal Records*. National Geographic Children's Books, 2015.

Websites

thekidshouldseethis.com/post/why-peregrine-falcons-are-the-fastest-animals-on-earth
Watch a video and find out more about how peregrine falcons are adapted to be the fastest birds on Earth.

www.cbc.ca/natureofthings/blog/winning-gold-animal-athletes-of-the-world
Learn more about some incredible animal athletes.

www.funkidslive.com/podcast/extreme-athletes-humans-vs-animals/#
Listen to some short podcasts about human and animal athletic ability.

Index

ants 5, 24–25

blood 8, 20, 27, 28
breeding 15

California sea lions 14–15
camouflage 13
cheetahs 4, 6, 8–9, 16
colonies 15, 25
Cuvier's beaked whales 26–27

diseases 28, 29
diving 5, 6, 26, 27

elephants 5
endangered animals 11
eyesight 6, 7, 8

fleas 4, 20–21
flexibility 4, 14, 15
flying 4, 6, 28

horned dung beetles 22–23

impalas 16–17

jumping 4, 16, 17, 18, 19, 20, 21

lungs 26, 27

mating 19, 23

octopuses 4, 12–13, 15
oxygen 27, 28

peregrine falcons 6–7
predators 13, 16, 17
prey 4, 6, 7, 8, 9, 10, 13, 14, 15

reproduction 11
Rüppell's griffon vultures 28–29

shortfin mako sharks 10–11
speed 4, 6, 8, 9, 10
spinner dolphins 18–19
streamlined shape 6, 10, 14
strength 4, 22, 23, 24, 25
swimming 4, 10, 11, 12, 15

wildebeest 4